CW00969034

GIFTS
from a
JAMAICAN
KITCHEN

Illustrated by
Joey Hart

Packaged by

D'MASKT

A Division of LMH Publishers

Published by LMH Publishing Limited
7 Norman Road
LOJ Complex, Building 10,
Kingston C.S.O., Jamaica
Email Address: lmhpublishing@cwjamaica.com

ISBN 976-8184-27-2

Book Design by Arlene Schleifer Goldberg
Illustrations by Joey Hart
Production by Zebra I. P.
Printed in China

INTRODUCTION

The food of Jamaica is reflective of the diverse culture of the country. Because the island is a sort of historical crossroads, the influences have been many, not just in cooking styles, but in the food and spices themselves. Some plants, like the ackee tree, came from West Africa; the breadfruit came from Tahiti; and the sorrel plant came from India. The list goes on and on. The influences of Africa, England, Spain, India and China to name a few, have contributed to the richness of the food and the culture.

In choosing recipes for this book, we tried to include, not only the traditional dishes, but also some variations that make use of local products.

Enjoy! Everything is irie!

APPETIZERS

Beef Patties ◆ 7

Cod Fish Fritters ◆ 9

Pepper Shrimp ◆ 11

Jerked Pork Snacks ◆ 13

Solomon Gundy ◆ 15

SOUPS

Goat Head Soup ◆ 17

Pepper Pot Soup ◆ 19

Pumpkin Soup ◆ 21

MAIN DISHES

Baked Black Crabs ◆ 23

Banana King Fish with Mustard Sauce ◆ 25

Roti with Chicken Curry ◆ 27

Beef & Mango in Beer ◆ 29

Chicken Cook-Up ◆ 31

Saltfish and Ackee ◆ 33

Escoveitch Fish ◆ 36

Octopus ◆ 38

SIDE DISHES

Johnny Cakes ◆ 34

Rice and Peas ◆ 40

Watermelon Marble ◆ 42

Callaloo Salad ◆ 44

Stuffed Breadfruit ◆ 46

Tropical Fruit Sala ◆ 48

DESSERTS

Rum Cake ◆ 50

Plantain Tarts ◆ 52

Banana Custard ◆ 54

BEVERAGES

Sorrel ◆ 56

Matrimony ◆ 58

Cool Mule ◆ 61

Jamaica Hop ◆ 61

Frozen Daiquiri ◆ 63

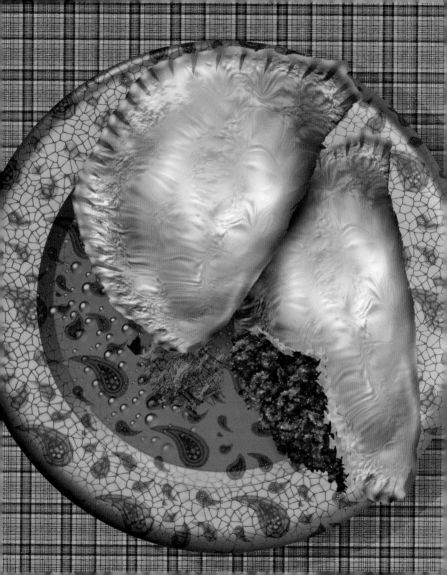

BEEF PATTIES

For pastry: Mix 4 cups flour and 1 teaspoon salt. Work in 1 cup shortening. Add only enough ice water to hold the dough together. Wrap in foil and place in refrigerator.

2 lbs ground beef
6 sprigs thyme
$\frac{1}{2}$ t curry powder
1 t salt
2 finely chopped scallion
1 finely chopped onion
1 t paprika
1 finely chopped pepper
1 T catsup

Saute meat, scallion, pepper and $\frac{1}{2}$ of the thyme until meat is brown. Pour off excess oil. Stir in remaining ingredients and simmer for about 30 minutes and cool completely.

Remove dough from refrigerator and roll out on lightly floured board. Cut dough into 4 inch circles. Fill half of the circle with the meat mixture. Fold over the other half and crimp edges together with a fork. Place patties on cookie sheet and bake at 400°F until golden brown, about 30 minutes.

COD FISH FRITTERS

The popular name is Stamp and Go!

$1/4$ lb salted codfish
$1/2$ c flour
1 minced onion
1 diced tomato
$1/4$ t hot pepper sauce
Juice of one lime
Cold water
Oil

The codfish should be soaked in water overnight. Drain. Wash codfish with lime juice. Dry the fish, shred it and remove skin and bones. Mix with onions and tomatoes. Add flour, hot sauce and water to make a batter. The mixture should be the consistency of thick pancake batter.

Heat oil in a skillet. Drop the mixture by spoonfuls into the skillet and press down so that the fritters are quite thin. Fry on both sides until golden brown and crisp. Drain on paper towel and serve warm.

PEPPER SHRIMP

Be sure to have a drink handy when you serve this spicy appetizer! The Scotch bonnet pepper is very popular in Jamaica. If you cannot find it, use any hot pepper.

1 lb medium shrimp
1 c white vinegar
1 onion, sliced
1 Scotch bonnet pepper
Salt and pimento grains

Boil shrimp in salted water for about three to four minutes—just until pink. Cool, peel and clean shrimp and set aside. Mix other ingredients in a small sauce pan and bring to a boil. Pour over shrimp and store in a covered container for 12 hours before serving.

Note: Pimento is sometimes called Jamaica All Spice in the U.S. and can be purchased whole or ground.

JERKED PORK SNACKS

There are many commercial jerk sauces and flavorings on the market, and they are all good, but you may want to try your hand at creating this special flavor.

1 boned leg of pork (3-4 lbs)
1 c vinegar
1 chopped Scotch bonnet pepper
1 finely chopped onion
2 cloves finely chopped garlic
2 T crushed pimento leaves
2 t pimento grains
1 t salt

Mix all the ingredients, except the meat, for the marinade. Cut pork into small pieces and place in marinade for 4 days, turning frequently. Keep covered in the refrigerator. Take out and wipe dry. Cook pork on the grill over burning coals to get a smokey flavor.

SOLOMON GUNDY

A popular appetizer when served with toast points or crackers.

$^1/_2$ lb pickled herring
$^1/_2$ lb pickled shad
$^1/_2$ c vinegar
1 T oil
1 T chopped onion
A few pimento grains
A few drops of hot pepper sauce

Soak the fish for three hours in water to cover. Pour off water and scald the fish with boiling water. Remove the skin, let cool, and shred fish.

Boil vinegar with onion and pimento grains. Add oil and pour over fish. Pack into jars and keep in the refrigerator.

GOAT HEAD SOUP

Also called mannish water!

1 goat head
1 lb pumpkin
1 lb carrots
1 cho cho
6 green bananas
1 lb yellow yam
12 small dumplings
1 chopped onion
Small piece crushed ginger
Salt and pepper
3 qts water

Prepare and clean goat head. Boil in water in a large soup pot. When meat is tender, remove bones and return meat to liquid. Continue to boil. Add other ingredients and simmer until vegetables are tender. Soup must be of thick consistency.

PEPPER POT SOUP

There are many variations of this soup on the island. This one has a few individual twists, and we think you will like it.

2 lbs chopped callaloo or spinach
2 qts water
1 lb soup meat
2 slices bacon or a pig's tail
1 lb shrimp, cleaned and deveined
1 doz sliced okras
1 minced onion
1 diced coco
Salt, pepper, herbs, hot pepper to taste

Place meat and bacon in a soup pot with water. Bring to a boil and simmer until meat is tender. Add callaloo, okra, coco and seasonings. Simmer until soup has thickened. You may remove the meat or leave it in as you choose. You can add small flour dumplings if you like and cook for an additional 15 minutes. Add shrimp last and simmer only until the shrimp turn pink.

PUMPKIN SOUP

You may not find coco in your market, but try substituting Irish potato.

2 lbs pumpkin
2 qts water
1 lb soup meat
3 stalks chopped scallion
1 small piece salt pork
1 chopped coco
$\frac{1}{4}$ t thyme
$\frac{1}{4}$ t salt
$\frac{1}{2}$ t hot pepper sauce

Place meat and salt pork in water and bring to a boil. Simmer until meat is tender. Remove the meats. Add peeled, diced pumpkin, seasonings and chopped coco. Simmer until vegetables are dissolved. Add seasonings to taste.

BAKED BLACK CRABS

6 black crabs, boiled
1 oz butter, softened
$\frac{1}{2}$ t black pepper
1 T chopped onion
1 country pepper, finely chopped
1 t vinegar
$\frac{1}{4}$ c fine bread crumbs
$\frac{1}{4}$ t salt

Clean the crabs and pick out all of the meat, including the claws. Save 4 shells.

Mix the crab meat with butter, onion, pepper, salt and vinegar. The mixture should be moist, but not soggy.

Wash the shells well and wipe with a little oil. Fill each with the crab mixture, top with the breadcrumbs and dot with butter. Bake at 375°F until the crumbs are brown.

BANANA KING FISH WITH MUSTARD SAUCE

King fish is plentiful in Jamaica, but you can substitute another firm fish such as grouper.

4 king fish steaks
2 ripe bananas, sliced
4 slices cheddar cheese
Salt and Pepper
Butter

Season steaks with salt and pepper and brown on both sides in butter. Remove them to a shallow pan and cover each with slices of ripe banana and top with a slice of cheese. Broil just until the cheese is melted and the banana is heated through. Serve with mustard sauce.

For the sauce, mix together until smooth:

4 T mayonnaise
4 T vinegar
4 T salad oil
1 t lime juice
3 t dry mustard
Salt and Pepper to taste

ROTI WITH CHICKEN CURRY

ROTI BREAD

Sift 2 c flour, 2 T baking powder and $\frac{1}{2}$ t salt. Add enough milk to make a stiff dough. Knead dough until smooth. Let stand for about $\frac{1}{2}$ hour and knead again. Divide into 4 balls. Roll out thin. Heat 1 T oil in a large skillet. Add the dough and cook covered for about $1\frac{1}{2}$ minute on each side. Remove and drain on paper towel.

CHICKEN CURRY

1 chicken, cut in pieces
1 medium onion, chopped
2 cloves garlic, chopped fine
1 Scotch Bonnet pepper, sliced
3 T curry powder
Salt and pepper to taste
2 c water

Brown chicken in oil. Add onion, garlic, pepper and seasonings. Add water a little at a time. Simmer for about 45 minutes. Remove chicken from pan and remove bones. Return chicken to sauce and heat through.

BEEF AND MANGO IN BEER

1 lb stew beef cut into small pieces
1 Red Stripe beer
1 c water
$^1/_2$ c mango chutney
1 t soy sauce
Pinch of salt and onion powder
$^1/_2$ c rice
1 c green peas

Combine first 6 ingredients in a casserole and bake at 350°F
for 1 hour. Add liquid to make a cup. Add rice and cook for
20 minutes. Just before serving, add the peas.

MANGO CHUTNEY

2 oz green ginger
2 lbs brown sugar
1 lb green mangos, peeled and sliced
$^1/_2$ lb raisins
1 T soy sauce
1 oz garlic powder and 2 oz salt
1 sliced hot pepper and 1 sliced onion

Crush ginger. Mix all ingredients and bring to a boil.
Simmer until chutney is thick and syrupy.

CHICKEN COOK UP

2 c rice
1 $\frac{1}{2}$ lbs chicken
2 small sweet potatoes
5 T Chinese sauce
3 cloves garlic
1 sprig thyme
2 c gungo peas
$\frac{1}{2}$ c oil
5 c coconut cream
1 small finely chopped onion
2 T brown sugar
Salt and pepper to taste

Cut chicken into small pieces and season. Cook gungo peas in hot coconut cream until tender. Brown chicken with sugar and onion. Add to cooked gungos. Add other ingredients and simmer for about 10 minutes. Add rice and cook at a low temperature until all moisture is absorbed.

SALT FISH AND ACKEE

Fresh ackees are not available away from Jamaica, but the canned ones are available in West Indian markets. This is a great Sunday breakfast dish when served with Johnny Cakes.

1 lb cod fish
1 large can of ackees
2 oz fried bacon
4 oz margarine
1 hot pepper, sliced and seeded
1 chopped onion
1 diced tomato

Soak fish overnight. Drain and discard water. Cover with cold water and bring to a boil. Skin, bone and flake the fish. Crumble the fried bacon and set aside.

Melt the margarine and stir in onions, tomatoes and pepper. Simmer 3 or 4 minutes. Add the fish and ackees. Heat through. Sprinkle bacon on top.

JOHNNY CAKES

When you serve these with ackee and salt fish, you have a wonderful Sunday breakfast.

2 c flour
2 T baking powder
1 t salt
2 t sugar
2 T shortening
Water
Oil

Mix flour, salt and sugar. Cut in the shortening. Add water, a little at a time. The dough will be sticky. Knead dough until smooth, adding more flour, if necessary. Make the dough into 2 inch balls. Fry the Johnny Cakes in hot oil until they are golden brown. Drain on paper towels.

ESCOVEITCH FISH

This dish can be made with any firm fish, such as snapper, king fish, or grouper. In Mexico, the fish is not cooked; it is eaten raw.

2 lbs fish filets
2 T oil
1 c vinegar
2 onion, sliced
2 T water
1 hot pepper, sliced
1 pimento leaf
A pinch of salt

Fry fish in hot oil and set aside. Mix remaining ingredients and bring to a boil. Simmer for 20 minutes. Lay fish in a shallow dish. Cover with hot vinegar sauce and marinate for about 12 hours before serving.

OCTOPUS

This delectable is called "Sea Pussy" by the local fishermen.

1 small octopus
3 T butter
Salted water to cover

Cut octopus into small pieces. Place in pot of salted water. Bring to a boil and cook until octopus is tender. Drain, dry and fry in butter. Serve with one of the following sauces.

PIQUANT SAUCE

Mix together: 1 T oil, 2 T vinegar, $1/2$ chopped onion and a pinch of salt and pepper.

CHEESE SAUCE

Melt 6 T margarine and blend in 6 T flour and 2 c milk. Stir over a low fire until thick. Add 1 c grated cheese and salt to taste. Heat until cheese is melted.

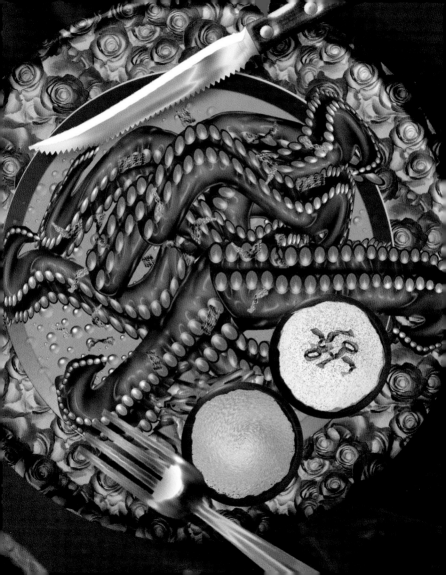

RICE AND PEAS

This dish is a national staple that is welcomed at nearly every meal whether you are serving fish, roast beef or chicken.

1 c red peas (kidney beans)
1 slice salt pork or beef
1 sliced onion
3 c rice
1 sprig thyme
1 grated coconut
1 T oil
1 sliced Scotch bonnet pepper
Salt

Soak peas overnight to soften. Saute onion with salt pork and seasoning. Add 1 c hot water to grated coconut and squeeze out cream.

Place peas and coconut cream in a pot with 2 qts water and cook until tender. Add salt pork and seasonings and cook for 10 minutes. Add rice and cook over low heat until rice is done. Add more water if needed to cook rice.

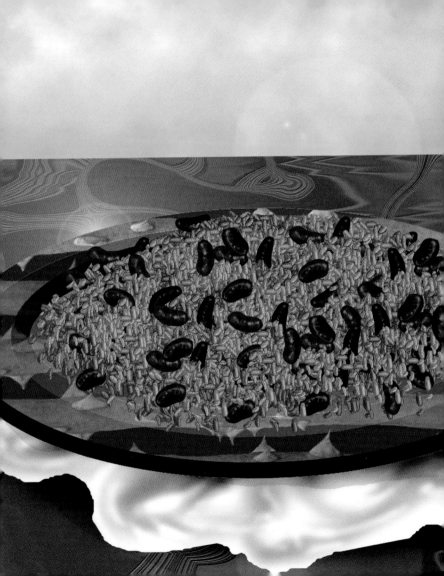

WATERMELON MARBLES

These make a smashing appetizer on a buffet table or they are
a refreshing dessert after a heavy meal.

1 watermelon
1 c rum
2 T sugar
Juice of 2 oranges

Cut the melon in half lengthwise. Remove the seeds. Use a
ball scoop to remove the flesh of the melon and put the melon
balls in a bowl. Keep the shell for a serving dish. Mix the rum,
orange juice and sugar and poor over the balls. Refrigerate for
at least 1 hour.

To serve, place a cocktail pick in each ball and pile on a bed of
ice in the melon shells.

CALLALOO SALAD

If your market does not carry callaloo, substitute spinach. Do not hesitate to experiment and add your favorite vegetables, such as tomatoes, mushrooms or scallions to this basic salad.

1 lb. callaloo
6 medium Irish potatoes
6 thin slices of cheese
$\frac{1}{2}$ c mayonnaise
Squeeze of lime juice

Boil the potatoes until a fork can pierce them easily. Drain and cool completely in the refrigerator. Slice.

Plunge the callaloo into boiling water for 3 minutes. Drain and chop.

Slice the cheese into $\frac{1}{4}$ inch strips. Mix all ingredients and dress with mayonnaise to which a squeeze of lime juice has been added.

STUFFED BREADFRUIT

This dish can make a complete entrée if you use your imagination.

1 medium breadfruit
1 T butter
$\frac{1}{4}$ c milk
1 small chopped onion
Pinch of salt

Roast the breadfruit for 1 hour in the skin. Roasted over charcoal is the best way, but it can be done over a gas burner.

Cut a circle in the top of the cooked breadfruit, scoop out the heart and discard, then scoop out the flesh and crush. Mix the flesh with the milk, butter and onion. Season with salt. To this mixture, you can add cooked ground beef, cod fish and ackee or left over stew. Pack the filling into the cavity, wrap with foil and warm through in a 350°F oven before serving.

TROPICAL FRUIT SALAD

This is a healthy treat that can be eaten every day. Change the fruit according to what is available.

1 pineapple
1 mango
1 papaya
1 orange
1 canteloupe
2 T brandy, optional

Cut off the top of a ripe pineapple. Scoop out the flesh and cut it in chunks. Mix with any or all of the diced fruits above. Toss with 2 tablespoons of brandy if desired. Return to shell and chill. Fresh lychee and mangosteen can be added for a surprise.

RUM CAKE

$\frac{1}{2}$ c butter
1 c sugar
3 beaten eggs
$\frac{1}{4}$ t salt
$\frac{1}{2}$ t baking powder
$\frac{1}{4}$ t mace
3 c flour
$\frac{1}{4}$ c milk
$\frac{1}{4}$ c molasses
1 t vanilla extract
2 c crushed peanuts
1 lb raisins
$\frac{1}{2}$ c rum
Pinch of soda

Cream together butter, sugar and eggs. Mix separately flour, baking powder, salt and mace. Add to butter mixture and mix. Add milk, molasses, soda and vanilla. Add nuts raisins and rum. Bake in a greased and floured bundt pan at 325°F for 1 hour and 10 minutes or until the cake tests done.

PLANTAIN TARTS

To make the pastry, cut 1 c shortening into 1 c flour until mealy. Add 1 c flour, 1 t cinnamon, $\frac{1}{4}$ t nutmeg and $\frac{1}{4}$ t salt and cut again. Add only enough water to form a dough. Wrap dough in plastic wrap and refrigerate for 1 hour.

FILLING

1 very ripe and finely mashed plantain
$\frac{1}{2}$ c sugar
1 T butter
$\frac{1}{2}$ t nutmeg
1 t vanilla
1 T raisins

Combine plantain, sugar and butter in a saucepan and cook thoroughly over a low flame. Remove from heat, add other ingredients and cool.

Preheat oven to 450°F. Roll out dough on a lightly floured board and cut into 4 inch circles. Spoon 1 T of filling into the center of each circle. Fold the dough over the filling and seal edges with a fork. Place tarts on a baking sheet, prick the top of each with a fork and bake about 15 minutes until pastry is lightly browned.

BANANA CUSTARD

Make this dessert more festive by serving it in a stemmed glass and topping it with whipped cream.

6 ox breadcrumbs
6 ripe bananas
3 c milk
1 T lime juice
$^{1}/_{2}$ c sugar
4 eggs
1 t nutmeg

Peel and crush bananas. Add lime juice and half of the sugar and nutmeg. Place in a buttered baking dish and cover with breadcrumbs. Beat eggs and the remaining sugar. Heat milk and add to beaten eggs. Pour mixture over bananas. Sprinkle remaining nutmeg over the mixture. Bake in a moderate 350°F about 30 minutes until custard is set.

SORREL

Sorrel is sometimes called 'flor de Jamaica'. This drink is especially popular around Christmas time.

3-4 bunches of sorrel
1 stick cinnamon
9 whole cloves
$^1/_2$ pt white rum
3-4 pieces of ginger
1 $^1/_2$ gal boiling water
4 c sugar

Strip the red blossoms from the stems of sorrel and place in a large pot with ginger, cloves and cinnamon. Pour on boiling water and leave covered for two days. Add sugar and rum to taste.

MATRIMONY

4 star apples
2 oranges
$^1/_2$ t grated nutmeg
6 T sweetened condensed milk

Wash fruits. Remove the pulp and seeds from the star apples.

Peel oranges and break into segments. Blend star apple pulp, orange segments and nutmeg. Add milk and chill for $^1/_2$ hour before serving.

Rum is a by-product of the sugar industry in Jamaica and the local drink of choice. Both of these drinks are made with a coffee liqueur that is also popular on the island.

*COOL MULE

$^1/_4$ cup Blue Mountain Coffee Liqueur
$^1/_4$ cup Rum
$^1/_2$ cup Vanilla Ice Cream

Blend the ingredients until smooth and frothy. Pour into a tall glass and serve.

*JAMAICA HOP

$^1/_3$ cup Blue Mountain Coffee Liqueur
$^1/_3$ cup Light Cream
$^1/_3$ cup Crème de Cocoa

Shake well with ice. Serve in a stemmed glass.

*Taken from *Caribbean Cocktails and Mixed Drinks* by Mike Henry

FROZEN DAIQUIRI

$\frac{1}{2}$ T sugar
$\frac{1}{2}$ oz lime juice
$1\frac{1}{2}$ oz rum
1 cup crushed ice

Blend together in an electric blender. Garnish with a slice of lime
or a sprig of mint. Serve in an elegant glass.
The recipe makes one drink.

ABBREVIATIONS

T = tablespoon	qt = quart
t = teaspoon	ml = milliter
c = cup	mm = millimeter
lb = pound	ġ = ġram

CONVERTING HOUSEHOLD MEASURES

From	To	Multiply By
Teaspoon	milliliters	4.93
Teaspoon	tablespoon	0.33
Tablespoon	milliliter	14.79
Tablespoon	teaspoon	3
Cup	liters	0.24
Cup	pints	0.50
Cup	quart	0.25
Quart	liter	0.95
Gallon	liter	3.79